TELL ME WHY, TELL ME HOW

HOW DO CHAMELEONS CHANGE COLOR?

MELISSA STEWART

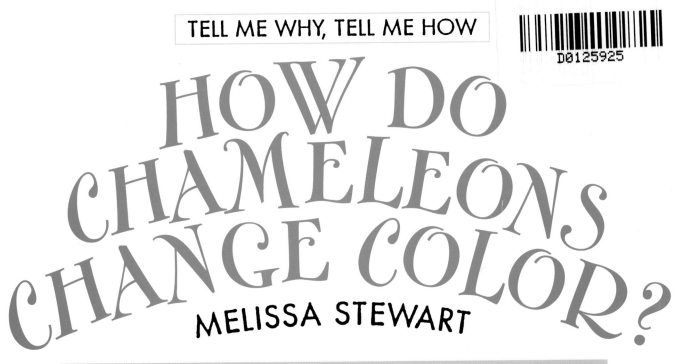

 Marshall Cavendish
Benchmark
New York

Marshall Cavendish Benchmark
99 White Plains Road
Tarrytown, NY 10591-5502
www.marshallcavendish.us

Library of Congress Cataloging-in Publication Data

Stewart, Melissa.
How do chameleons change color? / by Melissa Stewart.
p. cm.—(Tell me why, tell me how)
Summary: "Provides comprehensive information on chameleons and explains
how and why they change color"—Provided by publisher.
Includes index.
ISBN 978-0-7614-2922-7
1. Chameleons—Juvenile literature. 2. Chameleons—Color—Juvenile
literature. I. Title.

QL666.L23S89 2009
597.95-61472—dc22

2007024099

Photo research by Candlepants Incorporated

Cover Photo: DLILLC / Corbis

The photographs in this book are used by permission and through the courtesy of
Animals Animals: Stephen Dalton, 1; Joe Mc Donald, 4; Zigmund Leszczynski, 20. *Corbis*: David A. Northcott, 5, 15, 21; Frans Lemmens/Zefa, 8; Laura Doss, 22. *Minden Pictures*: Stephen Dalton, 6; Ingo Arndt/Foto Natura, 10, 19, 24; Piotr Naskrecki, 11; Frans Lanting, 12, 18; Michael & Patricia Fogden, 17; Pete Oxford, 23. *Super Stock*: Age Fotostock, 7. *Peter Arnold Inc.*: A. & J. Visage, 9. *Shutterstock*: 14, 25. *Getty Images*: Altrendo Nature, 16.

Editor: Joy Bean
Publisher: Michelle Bisson
Art Director: Anahid Hamparian
Series Designer: Alex Ferrari

Printed in Malaysia
3 5 6 4 2

CONTENTS

Veiled chameleons live in Saudi Arabia, a country in the Middle East. The colors and patterns on their skin help them blend into their leafy surroundings.

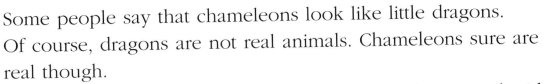
Some people say that chameleons look like little dragons. Of course, dragons are not real animals. Chameleons sure are real though.

A chameleon is a lizard. It has a plump body covered with tough scales and a large head with bulging eyes. Some chameleons have large, lumpy **crests** or colorful horns on their heads. Others have rows of spines running down their backs.

More than 130 **species**, or kinds, of chameleons live on Earth today. Most chameleons live in Africa or on a nearby island called

The Jackson's chameleon is also called the three-horned chameleon. It gets its name from the large pointed cones on its head.

Madagascar. They can also be found in southern Europe, India, and the Middle East.

Like other lizards, chameleons are **carnivores**, or meat eaters. Their favorite foods include locusts, crickets, mantids such as praying mantises, and other insects. Most lizards have no trouble chasing down their food, but chameleons move slowly. They rely on their super sharp eyes and their lightning-fast tongues to catch **prey**.

A chameleon's upper and lower eyelids are joined together, with just a tiny hole to see through. Their eyeballs can rotate in almost any direction—and they do not always

Faster than you can blink, a chameleon's tongue shoots out, catches its prey, and snaps back into the little lizard's mouth. When a chameleon gets thirsty, it munches on leaves.

move together. One eye can look up, while the other one looks down. One eye can stare straight ahead, while the other one glances over its shoulder. Because a chameleon can look

Now I Know!

What two body parts do chameleons rely on to catch prey?

Their eyes and tongue.

in two different directions at the same time, it can quickly scan its surroundings. This helps the little lizard spot **predators** as well as prey.

When a chameleon sees an insect, it attacks instantly. In one-fiftieth of a second, its sticky tongue shoots out, catches the prey, and snaps back into the lizard's mouth. A chameleon's tongue can be up to twice as long as its body. That makes the tongue perfect for catching hard-to-reach prey.

A chameleon's eyes are mounted on short stalks that stick out of its head. They slowly swivel up and down, right and left while the lizard's head and body stay perfectly still.

Some chameleons perch on branches close to the ground. Chameleons spend most of their time in lush forests, but sometimes they can be found in dry places.

Life in the Trees

Many lizards live in hot, dry places, but chameleons are most common in lush, tropical forests. Some chameleons spend their days on the forest floor. These chameleons have short tails, and tiny scales on the bottoms of their feet grip the ground. This helps the lizards move more easily.

Chameleons usually scurry along stems and branches. But sometimes they leap from plant to plant.

Most chameleons live in trees, however. A tree chameleon's long, curled tail is perfect for grabbing hold of branches. The lizard uses its tail like a fifth arm.

The bottoms of a tree chameleon's feet are smooth. They slide easily along rough branches. The lizard's **fused** toes look like the tops of salad tongs. A chameleon's foot has three toes on one side and two toes on the other, which allows it to grasp branches tightly and then shimmy along.

Even though chameleons have no trouble climbing through trees, they stay silent and still for most of the day. When a chameleon spots an enemy, it slowly sways back and forth with the breeze. The rocking movement helps the little lizard blend in with its surroundings.

Most tree chameleons are green, so they match the leaves around them.

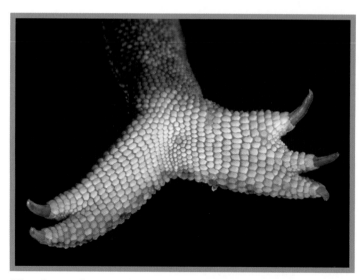

The feet of most chameleons are scaly on top and smooth on the bottom. Their fused toes help them get a good grip on tree branches.

This tiny chameleon looks a lot like the plant it is perched on. A hungry predator probably would not notice it.

Their skin is usually speckled, striped, or spotted. This characteristic also helps them blend in to the trees. This is called **camouflage**.

Chameleons are known for their ability to change color. Most species can go from green to brown and back. Some chameleons can turn almost any color, including red, blue, yellow, black, and even white. They can also change the pattern of speckles, stripes, and spots on their skin.

Most of the time, this chameleon is green. Dark colors like these usually mean the lizard is scared or cold.

Some other kinds of
lizards can change their
colors too, but not as fast
as a chameleon. A
chameleon can completely
change its appearance in less
than twenty seconds! And other lizards cannot turn a wide
range of colors.

While this lizard hid in the plants at the top of this picture, its green body blended into its surroundings. But now that it is resting out in the open, its body is slowly turning brown.

Warming Up, Cooling Down

An anole lizard's colors always match its surroundings.

If you have ever been to the southern United States, you have probably seen anole lizards scurrying across sidewalks or sunning themselves on rocks. When scientists first studied anoles, they discovered that these lizards can turn many different shades of green and brown.

They saw green anoles on leafy tree branches. They saw brown anoles on grayish-brown rocks. So they thought the lizards changed their colors to match their surroundings.

Later, scientists saw chameleons changing their colors too. They thought it was for the same reason. But now we know that anoles turn brown when they feel scared or angry. Chameleons change their colors for all kinds of reasons, such as a change in the amount of light around them. How do a chameleon's color changes help it survive? Read on to find out.

Like snakes, alligators, and turtles, lizards are **reptiles**. All reptiles are **cold-blooded**. Their body temperature changes as the air temperature around them changes. At night, a reptile's body cools down and all its body systems work slowly. Each morning, a reptile warms itself in the sun. When the animal is warm, its body works faster. It is easier for the reptile to move

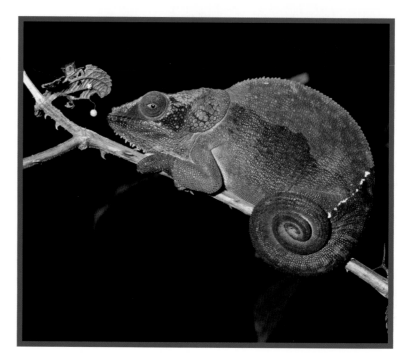

This chameleon's dark colors may mean that it feels cold.

16

around and to hunt for prey. By noon, a reptile might start to get too hot. It will then hide in a shady place and cool down.

When a chameleon is cold, it may turn a darker color. Dark colors **absorb**, or take in, heat better than light colors. This means a dark brown chameleon warms up faster than a light green one. In the middle of the day, warm temperatures and bright sunlight signal the chameleon to change its colors again. Now it may turn light green or even white to reflect the sun's sizzling-hot rays.

Switching colors gives chameleons an advantage over other lizards. They can spend more time each day at just the right body temperature for catching and **digesting**, or breaking down, food.

Now I Know!

How do a chameleon's color changes help it survive?

They help chameleons warm up and cool down.

When a chameleon gets too hot, its skin becomes very pale. This helps the chameleon cool down.

Since chameleons do not have ears, they communicate largely by changing the color of their skin.

Look at Me!

How do you let your friends and family know when you feel angry, scared, or excited? Most of the time, you probably tell them. You make sounds that form words. The words come out of your mouth, and the sounds reach other people's ears.

If you did not have a voice and other people did not have ears, it would be much harder to communicate. That is the problem chameleons face. Chameleons cannot talk, and they do not have ears. When they want to communicate, they use their skin to send messages and their eyes to receive them.

Chameleons cannot hear, but they have excellent eyesight. When they look at another chameleon, they can tell exactly how it feels.

When a chameleon feels scared or sick, it may turn dark brown or completely black. If a male chameleon spots another male in his **territory**, he may turn red, yellow, green, or blue. These bright colors send a message to the intruder: "Stay away, or I will start a fight." Most of the time, the enemy gets the message. He turns dull brown and slowly backs away. He is responding with another message: "Sorry, I did not know this was your space."

These male Jackson's chameleons have just run into one another. Compare their colors with those of the Jackson's chameleon shown on page five. Both lizards have turned very pale. Soon one will slowly move away.

When a male chameleon sees a female in his territory, he immediately flashes his brightest colors and most vivid patterns. "I am over here!" he is saying. "Would you like to mate?"

If the female likes the look of the male, she turns green or a pale color. If she turns black with yellow and blue spots, that is her way of telling him to get lost.

When a male Jackson's chameleon (left) comes across a female (right), his dark patches get even darker and some areas of his skin turn golden brown.

Why do some people have darker skin than other people? Because they have more of a natural pigment called melanin. Melanin is also responsible for the color of a person's eyes.

How Do Chameleons Change Color?

Human skin comes in many different colors. Some people have dark brown skin. Others have light pinkish skin. Still others have skin that is light brown or a little bit yellow.

What causes these differences? The credit goes to a **pigment**, or naturally colored material, called **melanin**.

Most of the time chameleons are green. This lizard's bright skin and tightly curled tail mean it is scared.

People with more melanin in their skin cells look darker than those people with less melanin.

A chameleon's top layer of skin is tough and colorless. It protects the lizard from scrapes and scratches. Below that are three more layers with different kinds of pigments. The second layer has cells with red and yellow pigments. The cells in the third layer contain materials that can make a chameleon look blue. The skin cells in the deepest layer contain melanin, just like human skin cells.

Most of the time, a chameleon looks green. That is because the lizard's second layer of skin contains large cells full of yellow pigment and small cells with red pigment. Cells in the chameleon's third layer of skin reflect blue light. When the blue light mixes with the yellow pigment, we see the color green.

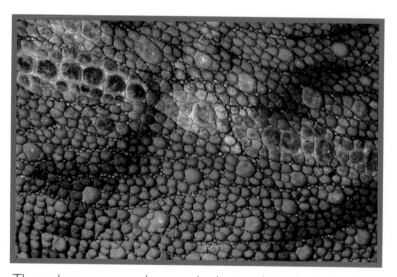

The colors we see when we look at a chameleon depend on the size of cells in different layers of its skin.

When a chameleon is cold or threatened, its brain sends a message to its skin cells. All the cells in the second and third layers of skin suddenly shrink. The dark color we see comes from the melanin in the chameleon's deepest layer of skin.

When a chameleon becomes aggressive or excited, its brain sends a different message to its skin cells. The size and

This chameleon is probably upset. It looks blue because all the pigment-containing cells in its second layer of skin have shrunk.

Now I Know!

Name a skin pigment found in people and chameleons.

Melanin.

shape of its skin cells begin to change. In some species, red cells expand and yellow cells shrink. These chameleons look red. In other species, both red and yellow cells shrink. These chameleons look blue. The colors look brighter or paler depending on the changes in the cells containing melanin.

Chameleons can change their body color in just a few seconds. That makes it possible for them to blend in with their surroundings most of the time. When chameleons get too hot or too cold, however, relief is just moments away. And when chameleons have something important to say, it is easy to get their point across.

Activity

To see why a chameleon turns a dark color when it feels cold and a pale color when it feels hot, try this activity.

1. On a sunny day, grab a pile of colorful construction paper and go outside.
2. Place pieces of black, red, pink, and white construction paper in a sunny spot. Put small stones on each corner so the papers will not blow away.
3. An hour later, place your palm on each piece of paper. Which one feels the hottest? Which one feels the coolest? Record your findings in a notebook.
4. Move all four pieces of construction paper to a shady spot. Add the stones so the papers will not blow away.
5. An hour later, place your palm on each piece of paper. Which one feels the hottest? Which one feels

the coolest? Record your findings in a notebook.
6. Look back at what you wrote. Based on your results, what color should a chameleon turn if it wants to warm up? What color should it turn if it wants to cool down?

Glossary

absorb—To take in.

camouflage—A disguise created by blending in with one's surroundings.

carnivores—Animals that eat other animals.

cold-blooded—Having a body temperature that changes as the temperature of the surroundings changes.

crest—A decorative piece on the head of an animal.

digesting—Breaking down food.

fused—Joined together.

melanin—A dark pigment found in the skin of many animals, including humans.

pigment—A natural material that gives an object or living thing its color.

predators—Animals that hunt and kill other animals for food.

prey—An animal that is hunted by a predator.

species—A group of similar creatures that can mate and produce healthy young.

reptiles—Animals with dry, scaly skin, lungs, and a backbone.

territory—The area where an animal lives.

Find Out More

BOOKS

Cowley, Joy. *Chameleon, Chameleon*. New York: Scholastic Press, 2005.

Lockwood, Sophie. *Chameleons*. Mankato, Minn.: Child's World, 2006.

WEB SITES

A Truly Bizarre Lizard

http://www.pbs.org/edens/madagascar/creature3.htm.

Animal Bytes: Got Questions?

http://sandiegozoo.org/animalbytes/gotq_chameleon.html.

How Do Chameleons Change Color?

http://www.opticsforteens.org/everyday/nature/chameleon.asp.

National Geographic.com: Chameleons

http://magma.nationalgeographic.com/ngexplorer/0210/articles/mainarticle.html.

Wildly Weird Creature Feature: Chameleons

http://www.rarespecies.org/kids/weird.htm.

Index

Page numbers for illustrations are in **boldface.**